Avril Lavigne

Ch JK

Wise Publications
part of The Music Sales Group

London/New York/Paris/Sydney/Copenhagen/Madrid/Tokyo

Published by
Wise Publications
8/9 Frith Street, London W1D 3JB, England.

Exclusive Distributors:
Music Sales Limited
Distribution Centre, Newmarket Road, Bury St Edmunds, Suffolk IP33 3YB, England.
Music Sales Pty Limited
120 Rothschild Avenue, Rosebery, NSW 2018, Australia.

Order No. AM967142
ISBN 0-7119-8472-7
This book © Copyright 2003 by Wise Publications.

Music arranged by James Dean.
Music engraved by Paul Ewers Music Design.
Printed in the United Kingdom by Caligraving Limited, Thetford, Norfolk.

Your Guarantee of Quality
As publishers, we strive to produce every book
to the highest commercial standards.
This book has been carefully designed to minimise awkward
page turns and to make playing from it a real pleasure.
Particular care has been given to specifying acid-free,
neutral-sized paper made from pulps which have not been
elemental chlorine bleached. This pulp is from farmed sustainable
forests and was produced with special regard for the environment.
Throughout, the printing and binding have been planned to
ensure a sturdy, attractive publication which should give years
of enjoyment. If your copy fails to meet our high standards,
please inform us and we will gladly replace it.

www.musicsales.com

Relative Tuning

The guitar can be tuned with the aid of pitch pipes or dedicated electronic guitar tuners which are available through your local music dealer. If you do not have a tuning device, you can use relative tuning. Estimate the pitch of the 6th string as near as possible to E or at least a comfortable pitch (not too high, as you might break other strings in tuning up). Then, while checking the various positions on the diagram, place a finger from your left hand on the:

5th fret of the E or 6th string and **tune the open A** (or 5th string) to the note (A)

5th fret of the A or 5th string and **tune the open D** (or 4th string) to the note (D)

5th fret of the D or 4th string and **tune the open G** (or 3rd string) to the note (G)

4th fret of the G or 3rd string and **tune the open B** (or 2nd string) to the note (B)

5th fret of the B or 2nd string and **tune the open E** (or 1st string) to the note (E)

E A D G B E
or or or or or or
6th 5th 4th 3rd 2nd 1st **Head**

Nut

1st Fret

2nd Fret

3rd Fret

4th Fret

5th Fret

Reading Chord Boxes

Chord boxes are diagrams of the guitar neck viewed head upwards, face on as illustrated. The top horizontal line is the nut, unless a higher fret number is indicated, the others are the frets.

The vertical lines are the strings, starting from E (or 6th) on the left to E (or 1st) on the right.

The black dots indicate where to place your fingers.

Strings marked with an O are played open, not fretted. Strings marked with an X should not be played.

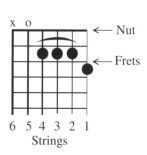

The curved bracket indicates a 'barre' - hold down the strings under the bracket with your first finger, using your other fingers to fret the remaining notes.

Anything But Ordinary

Words & Music by Avril Lavigne, Lauren Christy, Scott Spock & Graham Edwards

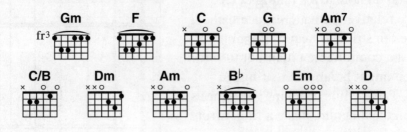

Intro   ‖: Gm | F | C | C :‖

Verse 1

   C   G
Sometimes I get so weird,

                   Am7
I even freak my - self out,

                  F
I laugh myself to sleep,

        G
It's my lullaby,

   C   G
Sometimes I drive so fast,

              Am7
Just to feel the danger,

I wanna scream,

       F   G
It makes me feel a - live.

Chorus 1

       F   **G**
Is it e - nough to love,

         C   **C/B Am7**
Is it e - nough to   breathe?

           F   **G**
Somebody rip my heart out,

   Am
And leave me here to bleed.

       Dm   **F**
Is it e - nough to die?

          C   **C/B** **Am7**
Somebody save my life,

           Gm   **F**   **Am** | **Am** |
I'd rather be anything but ordinary please.

Verse 2

   C   **G**
   To walk within the lines,

               Am7
Would make my life so boring.

             F
I want to know that I have been,

  G
To the extreme.

  C   **G**
   So knock me off my feet,

             Am
Come on now give it to me,

            F   **G**
Anything to make me feel a - live.

Chorus 2

       F   **G**
Is it e - nough to love,

         C   **C/B Am7**
Is it e - nough to   breathe?

           F   **G**
Somebody rip my heart out,

   Am
And leave me here to bleed.

      Dm   **F**
Is it e - nough to die?

       C   **C/B** **Am7**
Somebody save my   life,

         Gm   **F**   **Am** | **Am** |
I'd rather be anything but ordinary please.

        B♭   **Dm**   **C** | **C** |
I'd rather be anything but ordinary please.

Middle

  Am   **Em**
  Let down your de - fences,

          D
Use no common sense,

            G
If you look you will see,

            Am
That this world is a beautiful accident,

Em   **D**
Turbulent, succulent, opulent

        G
Permanent, no way,

     Am
I wanna taste it,

        C   **D** | **D** |
Don't wanna waste it away._____

Verse 3

(C)   **(G)**
  Sometimes I get so weird,

         (Am)
I even freak my - self out,

        (F)
I laugh myself to sleep,

    G | **N.C.** |
It's my lullaby.

Chorus 3

N.C. F   G
Is it enough, is it enough?

        C   C/B Am7
Is it e - nough to   breathe?

            F   G
Somebody rip my heart out

      Am
And leave me here to bleed.

        Dm   F
Is it e - nough to die?

            C   C/B Am7
Somebody save my life,

            Gm   F   Am
I'd rather be anything but ordinary please.

(Is it enough?)

        Dm   F
Is it e - nough to die?

            C   C/B Am7
Somebody save my life,

            Gm   F   Am | Am |
I'd rather be anything but ordinary please,   oh.

            B♭   Dm   B♭ | F | F | C   ‖
I'd rather be anything but ordinary please.

Complicated

Words & Music by Avril Lavigne, Lauren Christy, Scott Spock & Graham Edwards

Em	Cmaj7	G	D	Cadd9	C	Am

⑥ = D   ③ = F
⑤ = G   ② = A
④ = C   ① = D

Intro

Em Cmaj7
    Uh huh,

G D
Life's like this.

Em   Cmaj7   G   D | Em Cmaj7 ‖
Uh huh,   uh huh, that's the way it is.

G   D
 'Cause life's like this,

Em   Cmaj7 G   D
Uh huh, uh huh that's the way it is.

Verse 1

G
Chill out whatcha yelling' for?

Em
Lay back, it's all been done before,

Cadd9   D
And if you could only let it be you will see.

G
I like you the way you are,

Em
When we're drivin' in your car,

Cadd9   D
And you're talking to me, one on one but you've become,

Bridge 1

Cadd9
Somebody else round everyone else,

     Em
You're watching your back like you can't relax.

     Cadd9   **D**
You're tryin' to be cool, you look like a fool to me.

Tell me,

Chorus 1

Em   **C**   **G**
Why'd you have to go and make things so complicated?

  D
I see the way you're

Em   **C**   **G**
Acting like you're somebody else gets me frustrated

D
Life's like this you,

Em   **C**
   And you fall and you crawl and you break,

        G   **D**
And you take what you get and you turn it into

Am   **C**
Honesty and promise me, I'm never gonna find you fake it,

     G
No, no, no.

Verse 2

G
   You come over unannounced,

Em
   Dressed up like you're somethin' else,

Cadd9   **D**
   Where you are and where it's at you see,

You're making me

G
  Laugh out when you strike your pose,

Em
   Take off all your preppy clothes,

Cadd9   **D**
   You know you're not fooling anyone,

When you've become

Bridge 2   As Bridge 1

Chorus 2   As Chorus 1

Interlude | (G) | Em | Cadd⁹ | D   ‖

                    G
Verse 3   Chill out whatcha yelling for?
                Em
                    Lay back, it's all been done before,
                Cadd⁹   D
                    And if you could only let it be, you will see

Bridge 3   As Bridge 1

                Em   C   G
Chorus 3   Why'd you have to go and make things so complicated?
                    D
                I see the way you're
                Em   C   G
                Acting like you're somebody else gets me frustrated
                D
                Life's like this you,
                Em   C
                    And you fall and you crawl and you break,
                        G   D
                And you take what you get and you turn it into
                Am   C
                Honesty and promise me, I'm never gonna find you fake it, no, no

                Em   C   G
Chorus 4   Why'd you have to go and make things so complicated?
                    D   Em
                I see the way you're acting like you're somebody else
                        G   D
                Gets me frustrated. Life's like this you,
                Em   C
                    And you fall and you crawl and you break,
                        G   D
                And you take what you get and you turn it into
                Am   C
                Honesty and promise me, I'm never gonna find you fake it, no, no, no.

10

Get Over It

Words & Music by Avril Lavigne, Lauren Christy, Scott Spock & Graham Edwards

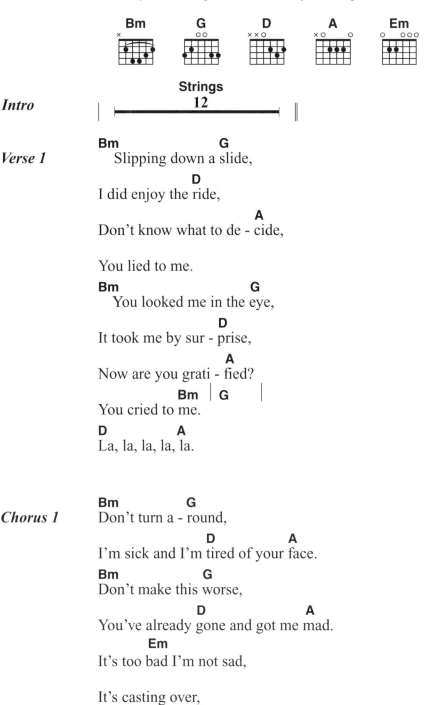

Intro

Strings
12

Verse 1

Bm   G
   Slipping down a slide,

       D
I did enjoy the ride,

            A
Don't know what to de - cide,

You lied to me.

Bm   G
   You looked me in the eye,

         D
It took me by sur - prise,

       A
Now are you grati - fied?

       Bm | G |
You cried to me.

D   A
La, la, la, la, la.

Chorus 1

Bm   G
Don't turn a - round,

           D   A
I'm sick and I'm tired of your face.

Bm   G
Don't make this worse,

           D   A
You've already gone and got me mad.

      Em
It's too bad I'm not sad,

It's casting over,

      G
It's just one of those things you'll have to get over it.

Interlude 1   ‖ **Bm** | **G** | **D** | **A**   ‖

Verse 2

Bm   **G**
   When I was feeling down,

                           D
You'd start to hang a - round,

                    A
And then I felt your hands all over me.

Bm   **G**
  And that was out of bounds,

                   D
You filthy rotten hound,

                  A   **Bm** | **G** |
It's better than it sounds, believe me.

D   **A**
La, la, la, la, la.

Chorus 2   As Chorus 1

Middle

G   **Bm**
Hey, yeah, you gotta get over,

G   **Bm**
Hey, yeah, you gotta get over it.

     Em
Too bad I'm not sad,

It's casting over,

    G   **(Bm)**
Just one of those things you'll have to get over it.

Interlude 2   ‖ **Bm** | **G** | **D** | **A** | **N.C.**   ‖

Chorus 3

Bm   G
Don't turn a - round,

                D   A
I'm sick and I'm tired of your face.

Bm   G
Don't make this worse,

               D   A
You've already gone and got me mad.

Bm   G
Don't turn a - round,

                D   A
I'm sick and I'm tired of your face.

Bm   G
Don't make this worse,

               D   A
You've already gone and got me mad.

      Em
Too bad I'm not sad

It's casting over,

    G
Just one of those things you'll have to get over it,

Em   Bm
   You'll have to get over it.

I Don't Give

Words & Music by Avril Lavigne, Lauren Christy, Scott Spock & Graham Edwards

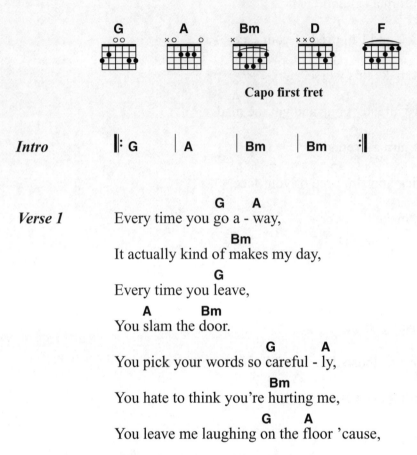

Capo first fret

Intro   ‖: G | A | Bm | Bm :‖

Verse 1

                G   A
Every time you go a - way,

               Bm
It actually kind of makes my day,

           G
Every time you leave,

    A   Bm
You slam the door.

                  G   A
You pick your words so careful - ly,

               Bm
You hate to think you're hurting me,

                G   A
You leave me laughing on the floor 'cause,

Chorus 1

     D
I don't give it up,

I don't give a damn,
G   **A**
What you say about that.
          D
You know I don't give it up,

I don't give a damn,
G   **A**
What you say about that.
          Bm
You know I'm not gonna cry,

About some stupid guy,
  G   **A**
A guy who thinks he's all that.

Interlude | G | A | Bm | Bm ||

Verse 2
                      G   **A**
I thought we were just hanging out,
             Bm
So why'd you kiss me on the mouth?
                G   **A** **Bm**
You thought the way you taste would get me high.
            G   **A**
You went to all your friends to brag,
         Bm
Guys are always such a drag,
         G
Don't you know the reason that I kissed you,
    A
Was to say goodbye.

Chorus 2   As Chorus 1

| | G   A   Bm |
| *Middle* | Hanging, hanging out, |

I am simply,
| G   A   Bm |
| Hanging, hanging out, |

I am simply,
| G |
| Hanging... |

| A   Bm |
| So why'd you kiss me on the mouth? |
| F   E |
| Don't you know that I... |
| D |
| I don't give a damn about you, |
| G   A |
| I would give it up not for you. |
| D |
| I don't give a damn about you, |
| G   A |
| I would give it up not for you. |
| Bm |
| I'm not gonna cry about some stupid guy, |
| G   A |
| A guy who thinks he's all that. |

| | D |
| *Chorus 3* | ‖: I don't give it up, |

I don't give a damn.
| G   A |
| What you say about that. |

| D |
| You know I don't give it up, |

I don't give a damn
| G   A |
| What you say about that. :‖ *repeat to fade* |

I'm With You

Words & Music by Avril Lavigne, Lauren Christy, Scott Spock & Graham Edwards

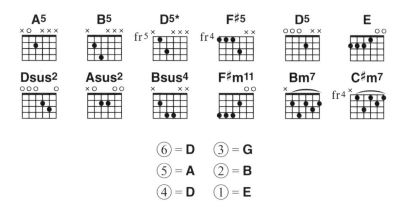

Intro   ‖: A5 B5 | D5* | A5 B5 | D5*   :‖

Verse 1

    F♯5
I'm standing on the bridge,

   D5
I'm waiting in the dark,

  F♯5   **D5**
I thought that you'd be here by now.

      F♯5
There's nothing but the rain,

   D5
No footsteps on the ground,

    F♯5   **D5**
I'm listening but there's no sound.

E   **Dsus2**
   Isn't anyone trying to find me,

E   **Dsus2**
   Won't somebody come take me home?

Chorus 1   **Asus2 Bsus4 Dsus2**
It's a damn cold   night,

                Asus2 Bsus4 Dsus2
Trying to figure out   this   life.

        Asus2   **Bsus4**
Won't you   take me by the hand,

       Dsus2
Take me somewhere new.

      F#m11   **E**
I don't know who you are,

    Dsus2   **F#5** | **D5** |
But I, I'm with you.

       F#5 | **D5** |
I'm with you.

       F#5
Verse 2   I'm looking for a place,

    D5
I'm searching for a face,

   F#5   **D5**
Is anybody here I know?

      F#5
'Cause nothing's going right,

    D5
And everything's a mess,

   F#5   **D5**
And no-one likes to be alone.

E   **Dsus2**
Isn't anyone trying to find me,

E   **Dsus2**
Won't somebody come take me home?

Chorus 2   As Chorus 1

   E   **Bm7**
Middle   Why is everything so con - fusing,

   E   **Bm7**
Maybe I'm just out of my mind,

      E   **Dsus2**   **C#m7** | **E** |
Yeah, yeah, yeah, yeah, yeah yeah, yeah, yeah, yeah, yeah.

Chorus 3

>   **A5**   **B5** **D5***
> It's a damn cold night,
>
>   **A5** **B5** **D5***
> Trying to figure out this life.
>
>   **A5**   **B5**
> Won't you   take me by the hand,
>
>   **D5***
> Take me somewhere new.
>
>   **F♯m11**   **E**
> I don't know who you are,
>
>   **Dsus2** | **Asus2**   **Bsus4** |
> But I, I'm with you._____
>
> **Dsus2**   **Asus2** **Bsus4** | **Dsus2** |
>   I'm with you._____
>
> **Asus2**   **Bsus4**
>   Take my by the hand,
>
>   **Dsus2**
> Take me somewhere new.
>
>   **F♯m11**   **E**
> I don't know who you are,
>
>   **Dsus2** | **Asus2**   **Bsus4** |
> But I, I'm with you._____
>
> **Dsus2**   **Asus2** **Bsus4** | **Dsus2** |
>   I'm with you._____
>
> **Asus2**   **Bsus4**
>   Take my by the hand,
>
>   **Dsus4**
> Take me somewhere new.
>
>   **F♯m11**   **E**
> I don't know who you are,
>
>   **Dsus2**   **F♯5**
> But I, I'm with you.
>
> **D5**   **F♯5**
>   I'm with you.
>
> **D5**   **A5**
>   I'm with you.

Knockin' On Heaven's Door

Words & Music by Bob Dylan

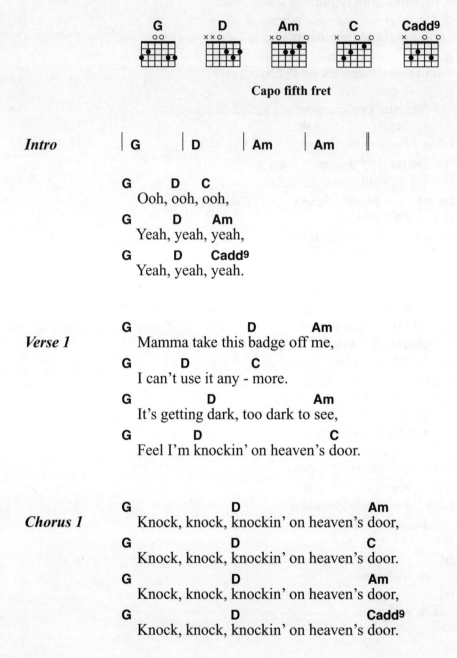

Capo fifth fret

Intro | G | D | Am | Am   ‖

G   D   C
Ooh, ooh, ooh,
G   D   Am
Yeah, yeah, yeah,
G   D   Cadd⁹
Yeah, yeah, yeah.

Verse 1
G   D   Am
Mamma take this badge off me,
G   D   C
I can't use it any - more.
G   D   Am
It's getting dark, too dark to see,
G   D   C
Feel I'm knockin' on heaven's door.

Chorus 1
G   D   Am
Knock, knock, knockin' on heaven's door,
G   D   C
Knock, knock, knockin' on heaven's door.
G   D   Am
Knock, knock, knockin' on heaven's door,
G   D   Cadd⁹
Knock, knock, knockin' on heaven's door.

Verse 2

G   D   Am
Mamma put my guns in the ground,

G   D   Cadd9
I can't shoot them any - more.

G   D   Am
That long black cloud is comin' down,

G   D   C
I feel like I'm knockin' on heaven's door.

Chorus 2   As Chorus 1

Outro

G   D Am
Yeah, yeah, yeah,

G   D Cadd9
Yeah, yeah, yeah.

G   D Am
Yeah, yeah, yeah,

G   D Cadd9
Yeah, yeah, yeah.

Losing Grip

Words & Music by Avril Lavigne & Clif Magness

Asus2   F%   Gadd9   F6sus2   Em(add4)   D5

⑥ = D♭   ③ = G♭
⑤ = A♭   ② = A♭
④ = D♭   ① = D♭

Intro   ‖: Asus2 | F% | Gadd9 | F6sus2 :‖

Verse 1

Asus2   F%   Gadd9 F6sus2
Are you aware of what you make me feel,   baby?

Asus2   F%   Gadd9
Right now I feel in - visible to you,

              F6sus2
Like I'm not real.

Asus2   F%   Gadd9
Didn't you feel me lock my arms around you?

F6sus2   Asus2
Why'd you turn away?

       F%   Gadd9
Here's what I have to say.

Bridge 1

F%   Asus2
I was left to cry there,

         F%
Waiting out - side there,

         Gadd9
Grinning with a lost stare,

       F6sus2
That's when I decided.

Chorus 1

Asus2 Em(add4) F6/9 Em(add4)
Why should I care,

Asus2
'Cause you weren't there,

Em(add4)
When I was scared,

F6/9 D5
I was so a - lone.

Asus2 Em(add4) F6/9 Em(add4)
You, you need to listen,

Asus2
I'm startin' to trip

Em(add4)
I'm losing my grip

F6/9 D5
And I'm in this thing a - lone.

Interlude

| Asus2 | F6/9 | Gadd9 | F6sus2 ||

Verse 2

Asus2 F6/9 Gadd9
Am I just some chick you placed be - side you,

F6sus2
To take somebody's place.

Asus2 F6/9
When you turn around,

Gadd9 F6/9
Can you recognise my face.

Asus2 F6/9
You used to love me,

Gadd9
You used to hug me,

F6sus2 Asus2
But that wasn't the case,

F6/9 Gadd9
Every - thing wasn't OK.

Bridge 2

As Bridge 1

Chorus 2

As Chorus 1

	D5 **F%**
Middle	Crying out loud,

Middle

D5   **F%**
Crying out loud,

       Gadd9 F%
I'm crying out loud.

D5   **F%**
Crying out loud,

       Gadd9 F%
I'm crying out loud.

D5 F%   **Gadd9 F%**
   Open your eyes,

D5 F%
   Open up wide.

Asus2 Em(add4) Fadd9 Em(add4)
Why   should I care,

       Asus2
'Cause you weren't there,

       Em(add4)
When I was scared,

F%
I was so alone.

Chorus 3

Asus2 Em(add4) F%   Em(add4)
Why   should I care,

       Asus2
'Cause you weren't there,

       Em(add4)
When I was scared,

F%   **D5**
I was so a - lone.

Asus2 Em(add4) F%   Em(add4)
Why   should I care,

   Asus2   **Em(add4)**
If you don't care and I don't care,

       F%   **D5**
We're not going anywhere.

Chorus 4   As Chorus 3

| **Asus2** |

Mobile

Words & Music by Avril Lavigne & Clif Magness

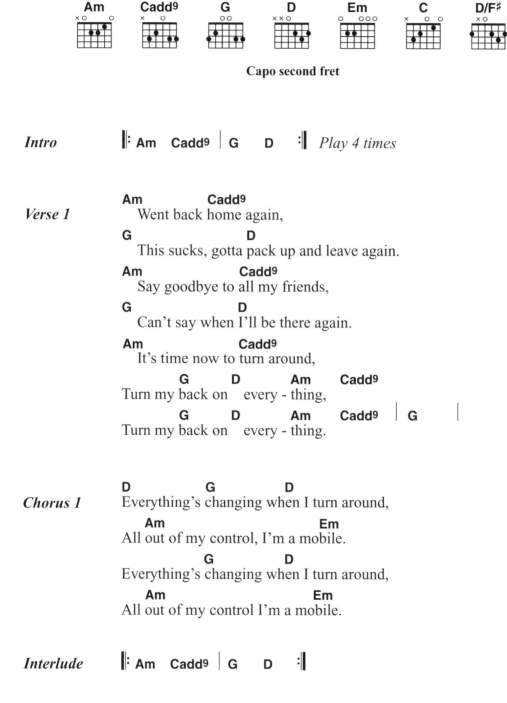

Capo second fret

Intro

‖: Am Cadd9 | G   D   :‖ *Play 4 times*

Verse 1

Am   Cadd9
Went back home again,
G   D
This sucks, gotta pack up and leave again.
Am   Cadd9
Say goodbye to all my friends,
G   D
Can't say when I'll be there again.
Am   Cadd9
It's time now to turn around,
        G   D   Am   Cadd9
Turn my back on   every - thing,
        G   D   Am   Cadd9 | G |
Turn my back on   every - thing.

Chorus 1

D   G   D
Everything's changing when I turn around,
     Am   Em
All out of my control, I'm a mobile.
           G   D
Everything's changing when I turn around,
     Am   Em
All out of my control I'm a mobile.

Interlude

‖: Am Cadd9 | G   D   :‖

Verse 2

```
      Am          C
      Start back at this life,
G                    D
      Stretch myself back into the vibe.
Am              C
I'm waking up to say I've tried,
            G                 D
Instead of waking up to a - nother TV guide.
Am              C
It's time now, to turn around,
            G       D         Am
Turn and walk on  this crazy    ground,
C        G
   Oh, oh,  oh, oh.
```

Chorus 3

```
D            G           D
Everything's changing when I turn around
     Am                    Em
All out of my control, I'm a mobile
                 G         D
Everything's changing out of what I know,
Am                    Em
Everywhere I go, I'm a mobile.
Am        Em
   I'm a mobile.
```

Middle

```
Cadd⁹                       D
      Hanging from the ceil - ing,
          Cadd⁹
Life's a mobile,
                            D
Spinning around with mixed feel - ings,
             C
Crazy and wild.
                 D/F♯
Sometimes I wanna scream out loud.
```

Guitar solo   ‖ G   ‖ D   ‖ Am   ‖ Em   ‖

26

Chorus 3

               G   **D**
Everything's changing everywhere I go,

    Am   **Em**
All out of my control.

               G   **D**
Everything's changing everywhere I go,

    Am
Out of what I know.

Em
   Yeah, yeah, yeah.

Bridge

G   **D**
  La, la, la, la, la, la,

La, la.

Am   **Em**
  La, la, la, la, la, la,

La, la.

G   **D**
  La, la, la, la, la, la,

La, la.

Am   **Em**
  La, la, la, la, la, la.

Chorus 4

               G   **D**
Everything's changing when I turn around

    Am   **Em**
All out of my control, I'm a mobile.

               G   **D**
Everything's changing out of what I know,

Am   **Em**
Everywhere I go I'm a mobile,

Am   **Em**
Everywhere I go I'm a mobile.

  | **G**   ‖

My World

Words & Music by Avril Lavigne & Clif Magness

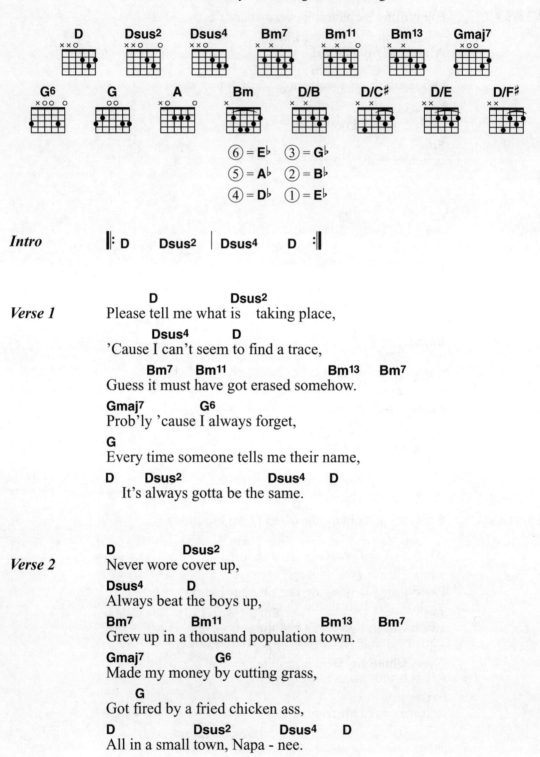

Intro   ‖: D   Dsus2 | Dsus4   D :‖

Verse 1

             D   **Dsus2**
Please tell me what is   taking place,

            Dsus4   **D**
'Cause I can't seem to find a trace,

          Bm7   **Bm11**   **Bm13**   **Bm7**
Guess it must have got erased somehow.

Gmaj7   **G6**
Prob'ly 'cause I always forget,

G
Every time someone tells me their name,

D   **Dsus2**   **Dsus4**   **D**
  It's always gotta be the same.

Verse 2

             D   **Dsus2**
Never wore cover up,

Dsus4   **D**
Always beat the boys up,

Bm7   **Bm11**   **Bm13**   **Bm7**
Grew up in a thousand population town.

Gmaj7   **G6**
Made my money by cutting grass,

      G
Got fired by a fried chicken ass,

D   **Dsus2**   **Dsus4**   **D**
All in a small town, Napa - nee.

Bridge 1

         A   **G**
You know I always stay

Bm
Up without sleeping,

        A   **G**   **Bm**
And think to my - self,

A   **G**   **Bm**
"Where do I be - long forever?

A
In whose arms, the time and place?"

Chorus 1

        G
Can't help it if I space in a daze,

       D
My eyes tune out the other way.

   G   **D**   **Dsus2**
I may switch off and go in a day dream.

G
In this head my thoughts are deep,

      Bm
Some - times I can't even speak.

      A
Would someone be and not pretend?

   G   **A**
I'm off again in my world.

Interlude 1 | **D**   **Dsus2** | **Dsus4** **D** ‖

Verse 3

    D   **Dsus2**
I never spend less than an hour,

Dsus4   **D**
Washing my hair in the shower,

  Bm   **Bm11**   **Bm13**   **Bm7**
It always takes five hours to make it straight.

       Gmaj7   **G6**
So I'll braid it in a zillion braids,

    G
So it may take all friggin' day.

      D   **Dsus2** **Dsus4**   **D**
There's nothing else better to do any - way.

Bridge 2

            A   **G**   **Bm**
When you're all a - lone in the lands of forever,

       A   **G**   **Bm**
Lay under the Milky Way.

A   **G**   **Bm**
On and on it's getting too late out,

  A
I'm not in love this time, this night.

Chorus 2   As Chorus 1

Instrumental | **G** | **G** | **D** | **D** | **G** | **G**   ‖

Middle

       D/B   **D/C♯**
I take some time, mellow out.

D   **D/E**
Party it up, but don't fall down,

D/F♯   **G**   **A**
Don't get caught, sneak out of the house.

Chorus 3   As Chorus 1

Chorus 4   As Chorus 1

Naked

Words & Music by Avril Lavigne, Curt Frasca & Sabelle Breer

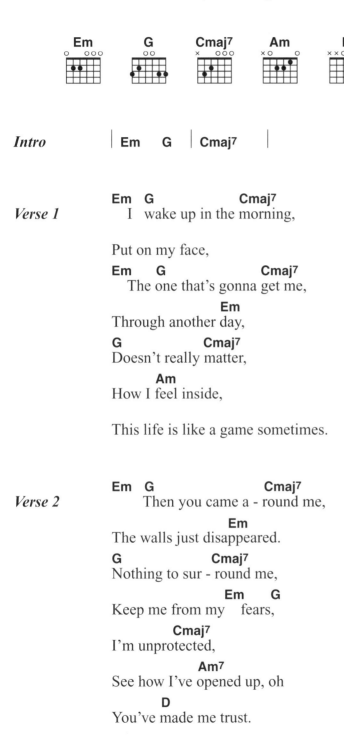

| Em | G | Cmaj⁷ | Am | D | C | Bm |

Intro | Em   G | Cmaj⁷ |

Verse 1

Em G   Cmaj⁷
  I wake up in the morning,

Put on my face,
Em   G   Cmaj⁷
   The one that's gonna get me,
                Em
Through another day,
G   Cmaj⁷
Doesn't really matter,
         Am
How I feel inside,

This life is like a game sometimes.

Verse 2

Em   G   Cmaj⁷
   Then you came a - round me,
             Em
The walls just disappeared.
G   Cmaj⁷
Nothing to sur - round me,
             Em   G
Keep me from my   fears,
        Cmaj⁷
I'm unprotected,
           Am⁷
See how I've opened up, oh
       D
You've made me trust.

```
            G        C        Bm      Am
```
'Cause I've never felt like this be - fore,

```
        Em
```
I'm naked around you,

```
        C
```
Does it show?

```
        G          C
```
You see right through me

```
          Bm     Am
```
And I can't hide.

```
        Em
```
I'm naked around you,

```
        C
```
And it feels so right.

Interlude | Em   G | Cmaj⁷ |

Verse 3

```
        Em      G            Cmaj⁷
```
I'm trying to remember,

```
                    Em
```
Why I was a - fraid.

```
        G
```
To be myself,

```
          Cmaj⁷                    Em
```
And let the covers fall away.

```
G                 Cmaj⁷
```
Guess I never had someone like you,

```
        Am           D
```
To help me fit in my skin.

Chorus 2

```
          G      C      Bm      Am
```
I've never felt like this be - fore,

```
        Em
```
I'm naked around you,

```
        C
```
Does it show?

```
          G          C
```
You see right through me,

```
          Bm     Am
```
And I can't hide.

```
        Em
```
I'm naked around you,

```
        C
```
And it feels so right.

Middle | **Em**   **D** |

Cmaj⁷ | **Em** **D** |
  I'm naked,

Cmaj⁷
  Does it show?

Em   **D**
  I'm naked,

Cmaj⁷   **Em**
  Oh, oh,

D   **Cmaj⁷** | **G** |
Yeah, yeah, yeah, yeah,

Cmaj⁷ | **Bm** **Am** |
  Oh, oh.

Em
Naked around you.

Cmaj⁷
   Does it show?

G   **Cmaj⁷ Bm**   **Am**
  I'm so naked a - round you,

        Em   **C**
And I can't hide, you're gonna,

             G   **C** | **Bm** **Am** |
You're gonna see right through,

            Em | **C** |
You're gonna see right through.

Outro   **G**   **C**   **Bm**   **Am**
  I'm so naked a - round you,

Em
And I can't hide,

   Cmaj⁷   **G**
You're gonna see right through baby.

Sk8er Boi

Words & Music by Avril Lavigne, Lauren Christy, Scott Spock & Graham Edwards

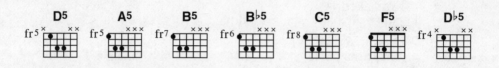

Intro ‖: D5 | A5 | B5 | B♭5 A5 :‖

Verse 1

D5　　　　　A5　　　　　　B5
He was a boy, she was a girl,

　　　　　B♭5
Can I make it any more obvious?

D5　　　　A5　　　　　　B5
He was a punk, she did bal - let,

　　　C5
What more can I say?

D5　　　　A5　　　　　　　B5
He wanted her, she'd never tell,

　　　B♭5
Secretly she wanted him as well.

D5　　　　　　A5　　　　　　　B5
　But all of her friends stuck up their nose,

　　　　C5　　　　　　　F5
They had a problem with his baggy clothes.

Chorus 1

　　　　C5　　　　　　　　B♭5
He was a skater boy, she said "see you later boy,"

　　A5　　　　　F5
He wasn't good enough for her.

　　　C5　　　　　　　　B♭5
She had a pretty face, but her head was up in space,

　　　　A5　　　　　B♭5 | B♭5 |
She needed to come back down to Earth.

Verse 2

D5   A5   B5
Five years from now, she sits at home
              B♭5
Feeding the baby, she's all alone.
D5   A5
She turns on T.V.
              B5
Guess who she sees?
           C5
Skater boy rockin' up MTV.
D5   A5   B5
She calls up her friends, they already know,
             B♭5
And they've all got tickets to see his show.
D5   A5   B5
She tags a - long, and stands in the crowd,
                 C5
Looks up at the man that she turned down.

Chorus 2

F5   C5   B♭5
He was a skater boy, she said "see you later boy"
             A5   F5
He wasn't good enough for her.
            C5
Now he's a superstar,
           B♭5
Slammin' on his guitar
               A5   F5
Does your pretty face see what he's worth?

Chorus 3

          C5   B♭5
He was a skater boy, she said "see you later boy"
             A5   F5
He wasn't good enough for her.
            C5
Now he's a superstar,
           B♭5
Slammin' on his guitar
               A5   B♭5 | B♭5   ‖
Does your pretty face see what he's worth?

Guitar solo | F5 | C5 | B♭5 | D♭5 | F5 | C5 | B♭5 | D♭5 A5 ‖

Middle

     D5   **F5**
Sorry girl but you missed out,

                          C5
Well tough luck, that boy's mine now.

                      B♭
We are more than just good friends,

        A5
This is how the story ends.

  D5   **F5**
   Too bad that you couldn't see,

                        C5
See the man that boy could be.

                      B♭5
There is more than meets the eye,

        A5   **D5**
I see the soul that is in - side.

Verse 3

  D5   **A5**   **B5**
   He's just a boy, and I'm just a girl

              B♭5
Can I make it any more obvious?

  D5   **A5**   **B5**
   We are in love, haven't you heard,

        C5
How we rock each other's world.

Chorus 4

  F5   **C5**   **B♭5**
I'm with the skater boy, I said "see you later boy,"

           A5   **F5**
I'll be back - stage after the show.

           C5
I'll be at our studio

           B♭5
Singing the song we wrote,

        A5   **F5**
About a girl you used to know.

Chorus 5

               C5   **B♭5**

I'm with the skater boy, I said "see you later boy,"

        A5   **F5**

I'll be back - stage after the show.

           C5

I'll be at our studio,

        B♭5

Singing the song we wrote,

      A5   **B♭5**

About a girl you used to know.

Nobody's Fool

Words & Music by Avril Lavigne & Peter Zizzo

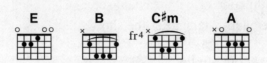

Intro   ‖: E | B | C#m | A   :‖

Verse 1

       E
Fall back, take a look at me and you'll see,

      B
I'm for real, I'll feel what only I can feel,

               C#m
And if that don't ap - peal to you, let me know,

             A
And I'll go 'cause I flow better when my colours show.

              E
And that's the way it has to be, honestly,

            B
'Cause creativity could never bloom in my room,

           C#m
I'd throw it all away be - fore I'd lie,

So don't call me with a compromise,

A
Hang up the phone,

                       (E)
I got a backbone stronger than yours.

Bridge 1

E
  La, la, la, la, la, la.

B
  La, la, la, la, la, la.

C#m
  La, la, la, la, la, la.

A
  Yeah, yeah, yeah, yeah.

Chorus 1

E
If you're trying to turn me

   B
Into someone else it's easy to see.

     C♯m
I'm not down with that,

A
I'm not nobody's fool.

E
If you're trying to turn me

   B
Into something else,

                           C♯m
I've seen it enough and I'm over that,

A
I'm not nobody's fool.

E   B   C♯m
  If you wanna bring me down go ahead and   try,

A   E
  Go ahead and try.

Verse 2

(E)
Don't know you think you know me like yourself,

   B   C♯m
But I fear that you're only telling me what I wanna hear,

Do you give a damn?

                  A
Understand that I can't not be what I am,

                  E
I'm not the milk and Cheerios in your spoon.

It's not as simple,

B
Here we go not so soon.

                  C♯m
I might of fallen for that when I was fourteen, and a little more green,

A   (E)
  But it's amazing what a couple of years can mean.

Bridge 2   As Bridge 1

Chorus 2   As Chorus 1

Middle | E | B |

C#m
Go ahead and try,

Try to look me in the eye,
              A
But you'll never see inside,

Until you realise.
    E
        Things are trying to settle down,
    B
        Just trying to figure out,
C#m
        Exactly what I'm about,
              A
If it's with or without you,

I don't need your doubt in me.

                E
Chorus 3   If you're trying to turn me
                    B
Into someone else it's easy to see.
                C#m
I'm not down with that,
A
I'm not nobody's fool.
E
If you're trying to turn me
                B
Into something else,
                        C#m
I've seen it enough and I'm over that,
A
I'm not nobody's fool.
E   B   C#m   A
    If you wanna bring me down go ahead and   try,   try.

Bridge 3   As Bridge 1

Bridge 4   As Bridge 1

            | E   ‖

40

Things I'll Never Say

Words & Music by Avril Lavigne, Lauren Christy, Scott Spock & Graham Edwards

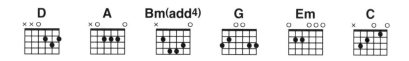

| D | A | Bm(add4) | G | Em | C |

Intro ‖: D | A | Bm(add4) | G :‖

Verse 1

    Bm(add4)   **G**
    I'm tugging at my hair,

              D
I'm pulling at my clothes,

                A
I'm trying to keep my cool,

          Bm(add4)
I know it shows.

             G
I'm staring at my feet,

               D
My cheeks are turning red,

              A
I'm searching for the words

       Em
Inside my head.

Bridge 1   I'm feeling nervous,

G
    Trying to be so perfect,

Em
    'Cause I know you're worth it,

A
    You're worth it, yeah.

Chorus 1

       D   **A**
    If I could say, what I wanna say,

                    Bm(add⁴)
I'd say I wanna blow you   away,

             G
Be with you every night,

                  D
Am I squeezing you too tight?

                   A
If I could say what I wanna see,

I want to see you go down,

Bm(add⁴)
    On one knee,

               G
Marry me to - day,

                      Em
Guess I'm wishing my life a - way,

C   **(D)**
    With these things I'll never say.

Interlude 1 | D | A | Bm(add⁴) | G   ‖

Verse 2

Bm(add⁴)   **G**
    It don't do me any good,

                  D
It's just a waste of time,

             A
What use is it to you

            Bm(add⁴)
What's on mind?

             G
If ain't comin' out,

                D
We're not going anywhere,

             A   **Em**
So why can't I just tell you that I care?

Bridge 2   As Bridge 1

Chorus 2   As Chorus 1

Middle
Bm(add4)   A   G
   What's wrong   with my tongue?

                            Bm(add4)
These words keep slipping away.

       A   G
I stut - ter, I stum - ble,

                    Em
Like I've got nothing to say.

Bridge 3   As Bridge 1

Interlude 2   ‖: D | A | Bm(add4) | G   :‖

                          Em
Guess I'm wishing my life a - way,

C   D
   With these things I'll never say.

Chorus 3   A
If I could say, what I wanna say,

                   Bm(add4)
I'd say I wanna blow you   away,

             G
Be with you every night,

                D
Am I squeezing you too tight?

                  A
If I could say what I wanna see,

I wanna see you go down,

Bm(add4)
   On one knee,

             G
Marry me to - day,

                    Em
Guess I'm wishing my life a - way,

C
   With these things I'll never say.

N.C.   D
These things I'll never say.

Tomorrow

Words & Music by Avril Lavigne, Curt Frasca & Sabelle Breer

G	Em7	Cadd9	D6/F#	Csus2	Bm

Capo second fret

Intro | G   Em7 | Cadd9 |

Verse 1

G   Em7
And I wanna believe you,

Cadd9   G
When you tell me that it'll be OK.

       Em7   Cadd9
Yeah I try to believe you,

But I don't.

G   Em7
When you say that it's gonna be,

Cadd9   G
It always turns out to be a different way.

 Em7   Cadd9
I try to believe you,

        G
Not to - day, today,

      Em7   Cadd9
To - day, today, to - day.

Chorus 1

Em7   D6/F#
I don't know how I'll feel,

    Csus2   Bm
To - morrow, to - morrow.

Em7   D6/F#
I don't know what to say,

    Csus2   Bm
To - morrow, to - morrow,

       (G)
Is a different day.

Interlude | G Em7 | Cadd9 |

Verse 2

     G   Em7
   It's always been up to you,

Cadd9
   It's turning around,

        G
It's up to me.

       Em7   Cadd9
I'm gonna do what I have to do,

       G
Just don't.

Em7
Gimme a little time,

Cadd9   G
   Leave me alone a little while.

Em7   Cadd9
Maybe it's not too late,

     G
Not to - day, today,

    Em7   Cadd9
To - day, today, to - day,   oh.

Chorus 2   As Chorus 1

Middle

G   Em7
  Hey yeah, yeah,

        Cadd9
Hey yeah, yeah,

And I know I'm not ready.

G   Em7
  Hey yeah, yeah,

        Cadd9
Hey yeah, yeah,

Maybe tomorrow.

cont.

G   Em7
  Hey yeah, yeah,
               Cadd9
Hey yeah, yeah,

I'm not ready.
G   Em7
  Hey yeah, yeah,
               Cadd9
Hey yeah, yeah,
                 | G | G   ‖
Maybe tomorrow.

Verse 3

G   Em7
  And I wanna believe you,
Cadd9   G
  When you tell me that it'll be OK.
       Em7   Cadd9
Yeah I try to believe you,
        G
Not to - day, today,
       Em7   Cadd9
To - day, today, to - day.

Outro

                     G   Em7
Tomorrow it may change,
Cadd9   G   Em7
  Tomorrow it may change,
Cadd9   G   Em7
  Tomorrow it may change,
Cadd9   G
  Tomorrow it may change.

Too Much To Ask

Words & Music by Avril Lavigne & Clif Magness

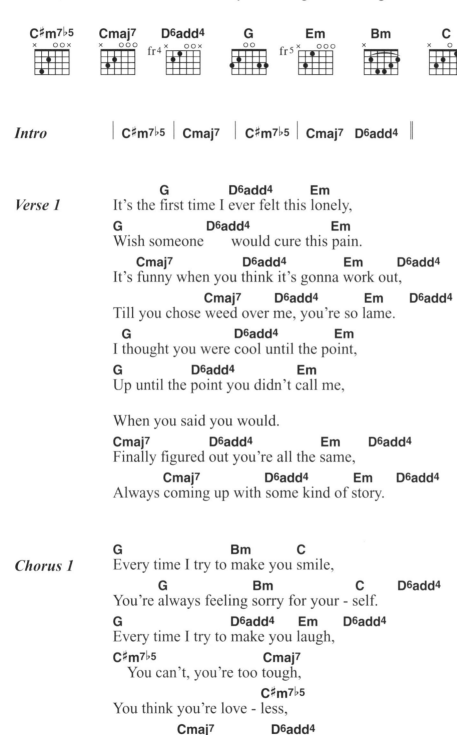

Intro | C♯m7♭5 | Cmaj7 | C♯m7♭5 | Cmaj7 D6add4 ‖

Verse 1

        G   D6add4   Em
It's the first time I ever felt this lonely,

G   D6add4   Em
Wish someone   would cure this pain.

      Cmaj7   D6add4   Em   D6add4
It's funny when you think it's gonna work out,

                Cmaj7   D6add4   Em   D6add4
Till you chose weed over me, you're so lame.

      G   D6add4   Em
I thought you were cool until the point,

G   D6add4   Em
Up until the point you didn't call me,

When you said you would.

Cmaj7   D6add4   Em   D6add4
Finally figured out you're all the same,

          Cmaj7   D6add4   Em   D6add4
Always coming up with some kind of story.

Chorus 1

      G   Bm   C
Every time I try to make you smile,

           G   Bm   C   D6add4
You're always feeling sorry for your - self.

G   D6add4   Em   D6add4
Every time I try to make you laugh,

C♯m7♭5   Cmaj7
  You can't, you're too tough,

                  C♯m7♭5
You think you're love - less,

          Cmaj7   D6add4
Is that too much that I'm asking for?

Interlude ‖: G   D⁶add⁴ | Em   :‖

          G   D⁶add⁴   Em

Verse 2   Thought you'd come a - round when I ig - nored you,

          G   D⁶add⁴   Em

Sort of thought you'd have the decency to change.

      Cmaj⁷   D⁶add⁴   Em   D⁶add⁴

But babe I guess you didn't take that warning,

       Cmaj⁷   D⁶add⁴

'Cause I'm not a - bout,

     Em   D⁶add⁴

To look at your face again.

          G   Bm   C

Chorus 2   Can't you see that you lie to yourself?

         G   Bm   C   D⁶add⁴

You can't see the world through a mirror.

G   D⁶add⁴ Em   G

It won't be too late when the smoke clears,

       C♯m⁷♭5   Cmaj⁷   D⁶add⁴

'Cause I, I am still here.

          G   Bm   C

Chorus 3   But every time I try to make you smile,

          G   Bm   C   D⁶add⁴

You'd always go on feeling sorry for your - self.

G   D⁶add⁴   Em   G

Every time I try to make you laugh,

C♯m⁷♭5   Cmaj⁷

   You stand like a stone,

          C♯m⁷♭5

Alone in your zone.

       Cmaj⁷   D⁶add⁴

Is that too much that I'm asking for?

Middle | C | Em |

C
  Can't find where I am,
Em
Lying here alone in fear.
C
  Afraid of the dark
    Em | F | F |
No - one to claim alone again.

Chorus 4   As Chorus 2

    G   Bm   C
Chorus 5   Every time I try to make you smile,
      G   Bm   C   D⁶add⁴
You're always feeling sorry for your - self.
G   D⁶add⁴   Em   G
Every time I try to make you laugh,
C♯m⁷♭5   Cmaj⁷
  You can't you're too tough,
                  C♯m⁷♭5
You think you're love - less,
      Cmaj⁷   D⁶add⁴
It was too much that I asked him for.

Outro   ‖: G   D⁶add⁴ | Em   :‖

Why

Words & Music by Avril Lavigne & Peter Zizzo

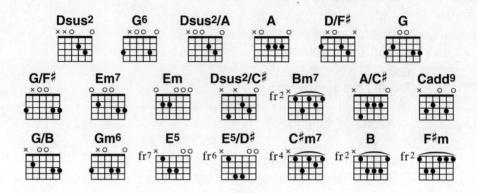

Capo second fret

Intro | Dsus2 | G6 | Dsus2 | G6 ‖

Verse 1

Dsus2   G6
Why

Dsus2/A   A
Do you always do this to me?

Dsus2   G6
Why,

Dsus2/A   A
Couldn't you just see through me?

Dsus2   G6
How come,

    Dsus2/A
You act like this,

      A   Dsus2
Like you just don't care at all?

 D/F# G   D/F#
Do   you expect me to believe,

       A
I was the only one to fall.

Bridge 1

    G   **G/F♯**
    I can feel, I can feel you near me,
Em⁷   **A**
    Even though you're far away,
G   **G/F♯**
    I can feel, I can feel you baby,
Em
Why?

Chorus 1

Dsus2   **Dsus2/C♯**
    It's not supposed to feel this way,
 Bm⁷   **A**
I need you, I need you,
G   **A**
More and more each day,
Dsus2   **Dsus2/C♯**
    It's not supposed to hurt this way,
 Bm⁷   **A**   **Em**
I need you, I need you, I need you.
A
Tell me,
Bm   **G**
    Are you and me still to - gether?

Tell me,
Bm   **Em⁷**
    You think we can last for - ever,
          G **A**
Tell me,

Why.

Interlude | **Dsus2** | **G⁶** | **Dsus2/A** | **G⁶**   ‖

Verse 2

Dsus2   **G6**
 Hey,

Dsus2/A   **A**
Listen to what we're not saying,

Dsus2   **G6**
 Let's play,

  Dsus2/A   **A**
A different game than what we're playing.

Dsus2   **G6**
  Try,

  Dsus2/F♯   **A**   **Dsus2**
To look at me and really see my heart,

    G   **D/F♯**
Do you expect me to be - lieve

        A
I'm gonna let us fall apart?

Bridge 2   As Bridge 1

Chorus 2   As Chorus 1

Middle

G
  So go and think about,

A/C♯
Whatever you need to think about,

       D
Go on and dream about,

Whatever you need to dream about,

Cadd9
 And come back to me,

     G/B   **Gm6**
When you know just how you feel,

  A
You feel.

Bridge 3   As Bridge 1

Chorus 3

Dsus2   **Dsus2/C♯**
   It's not supposed to hurt this way,

Bm7   **A**
I need you, I need you,

G   **A**
More and more each day.

Dsus2   **Dsus2/C♯**
   It's not supposed to hurt this way,

Bm7   **A**   **Em**
I need you, I need you, I need you,

Tell me.

Chorus 4

E5   **E5/D♯**
   It's not supposed to hurt this way,

C♯m7   **B**
I need you, I need you,

A   **B**
More and more each day.

E5   **E5/D♯**
   It's not supposed to hurt this way,

  C♯m7   **B**   **A**
I need you, I need you, I need you,

B
Tell me.

C♯m7   **F♯m**
   Are you and me still to - gether?

Tell me,

C♯m7   **F♯m**
   You think we can last for - ever,

       A   **B**
Tell me,

Why.

Unwanted

Words & Music by Avril Lavigne & Clif Magness

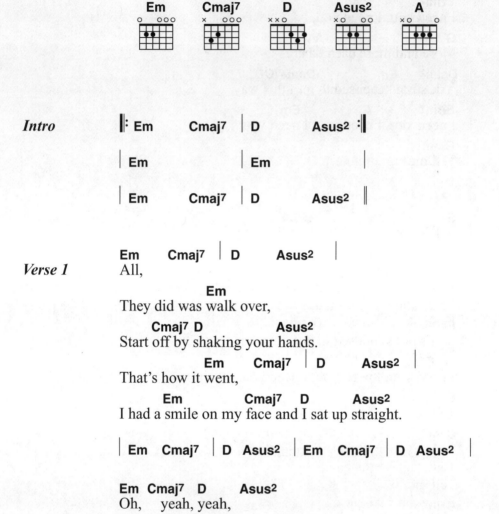

Intro ‖: Em   Cmaj⁷ | D   Asus² :‖

| Em | Em |

| Em   Cmaj⁷ | D   Asus² ‖

Verse 1

Em   Cmaj⁷ | D   Asus² |
All,

        Em
They did was walk over,

     Cmaj⁷ D   Asus²
Start off by shaking your hands.

         Em   Cmaj⁷ | D   Asus² |
That's how it went,

       Em   Cmaj⁷ D   Asus²
I had a smile on my face and I sat up straight.

| Em Cmaj⁷ | D Asus² | Em Cmaj⁷ | D Asus² |

Em Cmaj⁷ D   Asus²
Oh,   yeah, yeah,

  Em   Cmaj⁷
I wanted to know you,

  D   Asus²
I wanted to show you.

Chorus 1

Em
  You don't know me,

Cmaj⁷
  Don't ignore me,

D   A
  You don't want me there,

           Em   Cmaj⁷ |D   A |
You just shut me out._____

Em
  You don't know me,

Cmaj⁷
  Don't ignore me,

D   A
  If you had your way,

           Em   Cmaj⁷
You'd just shut me up,

D   Cmaj⁷ (Em)
Make me go a - way.

Interlude

‖: Em   Cmaj⁷ | D   A   :‖

‖: Em   Cmaj⁷ | D   Asus² :‖

Verse 2

Em   Cmaj⁷ | D   Asus² |
No,

        Em   Cmaj⁷
I just don't understand why,

     D   Asus²
You won't talk to me.

  Em   Cmaj⁷ | D   Asus² |
It hurts,

          Em   Cmaj⁷
That I'm so un - wanted for nothing,

      D   Asus² | Em   Cmaj⁷ | D   Asus² |
Don't talk words a - gainst me.

  Em   Cmaj⁷
I wanted to know you,

   D   Asus²
I wanted to show you.

Chorus 2

Em
   You don't know me,

Cmaj7
   Don't ignore me,

D   A
   You don't want me there,

           Em   Cmaj7 | D   A |
You just shut me out._____

Em
   You don't know me,

Cmaj7
   Don't ignore me,

D   A
   If you had your way,

          Em   Cmaj7
You'd just shut me up,

D   Cmaj7 Em   Cmaj7
Make me go a - way.

D   A | Em Cmaj7 | D   A |
Make me go a - way.

Middle

Em   Cmaj7
   I tried to belong,

        D
It didn't seem wrong,

A   Em   Cmaj7 | D   A |
   My head aches,

Em   Cmaj7
   It's been so long,

        D
I'll write this song,

A   Em   Cmaj7 | D | D |
   If that's what it takes.

Chorus 3   As Chorus 1

Chorus 4   As Chorus 2

Outro |Em   Cmaj7 |

D   A
   Make me go away.

| Em   Cmaj7 | D   A ‖